POPULAR CULTURE

A VIEW FROM THE PAPARAZZI

Orlando Bloom	John Legend
Kelly Clarkson	Lindsay Lohan
Johnny Depp	Mandy Moore
Hilary Duff	Ashlee and Jessica Simpson
Will Ferrell	
Jake Gyllenhaal	Justin Timberlake
Paris and Nicky Hilton	Owen and Luke Wilson
LeBron James	Tiger Woods

LeBron James

Hal Marcovitz

Mason Crest Publishers

LeBron James

FRONTIS

LeBron James has emerged as one of the NBA's best young players, leading his team to the NBA Finals in 2007.

Produced by 21st Century Publishing and Communications, Inc.

MASON CREST PUBLISHERS INC.
370 Reed Road
Broomall, Pennsylvania 19008
(866) MCP-BOOK (toll free)
www.masoncrest.com

Printed in the United States.

First Printing

9 8 7 6 5 4 3 2 1

Library of Congress Cataloging-in-Publication Data

Marcovitz, Hal.
 LeBron James / Hal Marcovitz.
   p. cm.—(Pop culture: a view from the papparazzi)
 Includes bibliographical references and index.
 Hardback edition: ISBN-13: 978-1-4222-0205-0
 Paperback edition: ISBN-13: 978-1-4222-0359-0
 1. James, LeBron—Juvenile literature. 2. Basketball players—United States—Biography—Juvenile literature. I. Title.
GV884.J36M37 2008
796.323092—dc22
[B]   2007008989

CONTENTS

LeBron James drops in two of his 45 points during the Cleveland Cavaliers' 121–120 playoff victory over the Washington Wizards, May 2006. LeBron scored the game-winning basket with less than a second remaining. "I felt like it shouldn't have gone to overtime," he told reporters afterward. "I made a move and I was able to get to the baseline."

1

King James

With the final seconds of the game ticking away, LeBron James drove toward the basket past three players for the Washington Wizards. He leaped over all three defenders, who were stunned by his strength, quickness, and desire. Reaching the basket, James let the ball roll gently off his fingertips into the rim.

Less than a second after the ball dropped through the hoop, the buzzer sounded to end the game. LeBron's last-second heroics had lifted his team, the Cleveland Cavaliers, to victory in the fifth game of the Cavs' NBA playoff series against the Wizards by a final score of 121 to 120.

The more than 20,000 fans jammed into Cleveland's Quicken Loans Arena on that May night in 2006 shot to their feet and nearly raised the ceiling with their cheers. When the series against the Wizards had begun just a few days earlier, it had marked the first time in eight years that Cleveland had made the NBA playoffs. And now, thanks to LeBron's heroics on the court, the Cavaliers held a three-games-to-two advantage over the Wizards in the playoff series.

Amazing Talent

LeBron is one of the most celebrated young athletes to enter the NBA in years, and so far he has lived up to the team's expectations. LeBron did more than just sink the final shot to win the playoff game; he dominated the game all night. Cavaliers coach Mike Brown told the *New York Times*:

> **"It was not just that last shot. He was 17 for 18 from the free-throw line, and we needed every single point. He had five offensive rebounds. He's an amazing guy and an amazing talent."**

Since the late 1990s the Cavaliers had been one of the NBA's worst teams. After finishing with a record of just 17 wins and 65 losses in the 2002–03 season, the Cavs were awarded the top pick in the NBA **draft**. The team used the pick to select LeBron, who had passed up college to enter the NBA after an outstanding high school career.

The last time the Cavaliers had made the NBA playoffs, it was 1998 and LeBron was just 13 years old. During his first two seasons with the Cavs, the team improved steadily. Cleveland fans were finally rewarded for their patience in the 2005–06 season, when LeBron led the Cavaliers to a 50–32 record and a playoff berth. Shortly before the playoffs started, LeBron told a reporter for *USA Today*:

> **"I think it was time. I was so used to going out and winning state championships and playing in the post-season. This just shows how much I have grown and how much our organization has grown. It was tough to watch [the playoffs] the first two years. I won't be watching this time. I'll be part of it."**

LeBron and his teammates celebrate with their fans after winning the fifth game of their 2006 playoff series against the Wizards. The victory enabled Cleveland to take a three-games-to-two lead in the series. The Cavaliers won the next game against the Wizards to advance to the second round of the 2006 playoffs.

Playoff Run

Because of LeBron's leadership and great play, the Cavaliers would go on to win their first playoff series, defeating the Wizards four games to two. However, in the next round Cleveland faced a much tougher opponent: the seasoned Detroit Pistons. Led by superstar Rasheed Wallace, the Pistons had won the NBA title in 2004, then played in the finals again in 2005 before losing to the San Antonio Spurs in the final game of a seven-game series. In the 2006 playoffs, the Pistons were favored to return to the NBA finals. But now LeBron and the upstart Cavaliers stood in their way.

Before the series began, Wallace even boasted that the Pistons would quickly take care of the Cavaliers and advance to the next round. Things would not turn out exactly as Wallace predicted, however. Instead of easily sweeping aside the Cavaliers, LeBron's team gave the Pistons all they could handle. After dropping the first two games in the

Pistons' power forward Rasheed Wallace (left) battles with LeBron for the ball, May 2006. Wallace had predicted a quick Detroit victory in their second-round playoff series, but LeBron and the Cavaliers put up a strong fight. They tied the series at two wins apiece when LeBron scored 22 points, including two key free throws with just seconds remaining.

series to Detroit, the Cavaliers clawed their way back into contention by winning the next two games. Then the Cavs shocked the Pistons by taking the fifth game in the series. With one more win, the Cavaliers would eliminate the Pistons and advance to the next round.

During the series, LeBron told a reporter for the Associated Press that the Pistons did not intimidate him:

> **"Everybody was counting us out. Even people in our own backyard were counting us out. That's extra motivation for us. We don't listen to nobody."**

Power Franchise

The series would go to the full seven games before ending in a Detroit victory. Down three games to two and facing elimination from the playoffs, Wallace and the other Pistons won the final two games in the series and advanced to the next round—which they lost to the Miami Heat, the eventual NBA champs.

As for the Cavaliers, although LeBron's team lost the series the young star's performance in the playoffs had been stellar. His efforts helped give the Cleveland players some much-needed playoff experience, which their coaches hoped would lay a foundation for future playoff runs. By the end of the 2005–06 season, LeBron had established the Cavaliers as one of the NBA's best teams.

The Cavaliers' quick rise and dramatic playoff run showed that the team had made the right decision when it drafted LeBron right out of high school. Shortly after joining the Cavaliers and signing a multimillion dollar contract, the press labeled the former high school player "King James." Obviously, the people of Cleveland expected a lot out of the young player. And as his performance in the playoffs proved, King James was now ready to deliver.

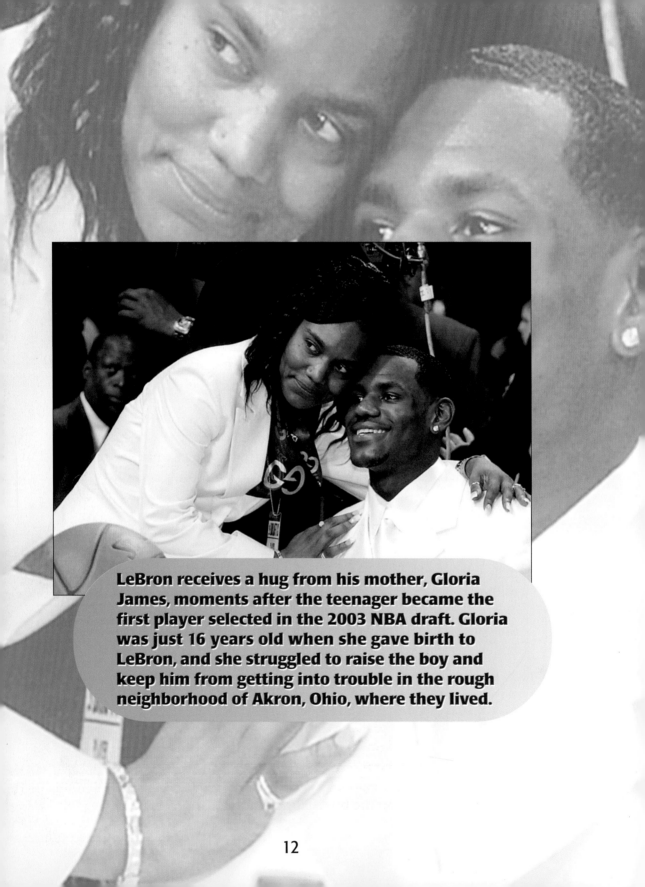

LeBron receives a hug from his mother, Gloria James, moments after the teenager became the first player selected in the 2003 NBA draft. Gloria was just 16 years old when she gave birth to LeBron, and she struggled to raise the boy and keep him from getting into trouble in the rough neighborhood of Akron, Ohio, where they lived.

2

The Chosen One

In 1987, when LeBron James was nearly three years old, his mother, Gloria James, gave him a toy basketball set for Christmas. At the time, LeBron and his mother were living with her mother Freda on Hickory Street in Akron, Ohio. The boy was so excited that he started playing with the basketball set immediately.

As LeBron tried to dunk the basketball, he had no way of knowing that a tragedy had occurred in his family. His grandmother Freda had died earlier that morning. Gloria decided not to tell LeBron because she did not want to spoil the boy's Christmas.

LeBron was born when Gloria was 16 years old. He never knew his father, but his mother's boyfriend, Eddie Jackson, was a regular visitor to the James home and often served as a father figure for little "Bron Bron." Jackson was by Gloria's side on that Christmas morning, and he later recalled watching LeBron play with the toy basketball set. In an interview with author David Lee Morgan Jr., Jackson recalled how LeBron immediately started dunking the ball into the hoop:

> **"Me and Gloria are looking at him run that thing over, so we raised it up so he would start shooting at it, instead of knocking the thing over. But all he would do is start back from the living room, run through the dining room and he was still dunking the ball. I was thinking, *man this kid has some elevation for just being three years old.*"**

Elizabeth Park

With the death of her mother, and without a husband to support her, Gloria was soon forced to find a new home along with LeBron and Gloria's two brothers, Terry, 22, and Curt, 12. The Jameses moved in with friends in a tough Akron public housing project known as Elizabeth Park. Crime was rampant in the community. Drugs were sold on the streets. Gang fights and drive-by shootings were common. Later, LeBron told Morgan:

> **"Anybody who knows about Elizabeth Park knows how bad it is. You had gunshots flying and cop cars driving around there all the time. As a young boy, it was scary but I never got into none of that stuff. That just wasn't me. . . . I knew it was wrong."**

Terry and Curt soon moved out, but Gloria and LeBron lived in Elizabeth Park for six years. They never had a home of their own. Instead, they were constantly on the move, always living with friends who could offer a spare room to the young mother and her son. One year Gloria and LeBron moved seven times.

It was a difficult time for Gloria and LeBron. Money was tight and Gloria occasionally found herself in scrapes with the police. Meanwhile, LeBron started school but he became a habitual **truant**.

A model of the toy basketball set that LeBron James received as a gift from his mother when he was three years old is on display at the LeBron James store and museum in SoHo, New York. "LeBron would be in his diaper, dunking all over that rim," his uncle Terry James later recalled.

In the fourth grade, he missed 87 days of school. LeBron spent the time mostly wandering around the neighborhood, watching the older boys play basketball and football in the streets.

South Rangers Tailback

LeBron enjoyed playing pickup games in the street himself, but when he was nine years old he discovered organized sports. One of his mother's former boyfriends, Bruce Kelker, had started coaching the local youth football team, known as the South Rangers. He had seen LeBron around the neighborhood, knew he had problems in school, and felt the boy could benefit from the **discipline** required by organized sports. Kelker invited him to join the team. It was clear from the first time LeBron touched the ball that he was a natural and gifted athlete. Kelker told Morgan:

> **"LeBron had done nothing but play street ball. He had never played organized ball, and when we got him on the field, I'll tell you, I had never coached a kid who picked up the knowledge of the game so quick."**

LeBron played **tailback** for the South Rangers. In his first year with the team, he scored an astounding 18 touchdowns in a six-game season. Meanwhile, Gloria realized her son needed to pay more attention to his school work. As LeBron neared the end of his fourth-grade year, Gloria worked with him to complete all the school assignments he had missed because of his absences. Despite her work with the boy, Gloria decided that LeBron needed more guidance than she could provide. She approached a friend, Frank Walker, and asked him to take her son into his home.

Perfect Attendance

Frank and his wife Pam were already the parents of three young children, including one of LeBron's best friends, Frankie Walker Jr. The Walkers made the sacrifice, though, and accepted LeBron into their home. For LeBron, the Walkers would provide a stable home environment, the discipline he needed to pay attention to his studies, and a path to his future acclaim as one of the nation's most accomplished basketball players.

LeBron's first experience with organized sports was in a youth football league. He later said, "The South Rangers meant a lot to me. All the coaches and the parents really cared about us, and they made playing the game fun. I actually wanted to play in the NFL because of my experience playing for the Rangers."

After moving into the Walker home, LeBron's life changed drastically. Although he was used to sleeping in, he soon learned that in the Walker home the day started just past 6 A.M. LeBron's chores included cleaning the bathroom. He was expected to do his homework every day and be in bed by a specific time.

LeBron worked hard, and the change in his life soon started to become evident. In the fifth grade, LeBron registered perfect attendance for the year, and over the next few years he would become a good student. Later, LeBron told Morgan:

> **"It was like a new beginning for me. When I moved in with the Walkers, I went from missing 87 days my fourth-grade year to zero days in the fifth grade. [The Walkers] all may not know how much I care about them, but I care about them a lot. I love them. They are like my family too, and I wouldn't be here without them."**

Frank Walker also taught LeBron how to play basketball. LeBron proved to have a natural talent for the sport. He soon joined a local team, the Northeast Ohio Shooting Stars. His coach, Dru Joyce II, later

Dru Joyce II, shown here speaking to reporters after a game, was both LeBron's coach and the father of one of his best friends. He appreciated LeBron's willingness to work hard to make himself a better player. LeBron and his teammates on the Northeast Ohio Shooting Stars dominated their league for several years, nearly winning a national championship.

said that he was impressed with LeBron's desire, work ethic, and raw athletic talent:

> **"LeBron has those kinds of things every coach wishes they could take credit for, but you just can't. All I can say is, we kept him busy, kept him out of the streets, showed him what we knew, and [he] sucked it up like [a sponge]. . . . Even as a young kid . . . he never missed a practice. I mean, he always wanted to be in the gym. He's always wanted to learn."**

Fab Four

LeBron eventually became so good that he was able to play against, and beat, much older boys. When he was in the sixth grade, his principal at Riedinger Middle School in Akron caught him cutting class so he could play against eighth-graders during their lunch break. Before breaking up the game, the principal was stunned as he watched LeBron dominate the bigger and older boys.

LeBron made three good friends on the Shooting Stars: Sian Cotton, Willie Magee, and Dru Joyce III, the coach's son. All four boys were excellent players—they called themselves the "Fab Four"—and they led the team to many victories. From the ages of 11 to 14, the four boys led the Shooting Stars to the national Amateur Athletic Union competitions, each year placing in the top ten finishers. In their last year together on the Shooting Stars, LeBron and the others led the team to the championship game, which they lost by two points to a team that had won the national title four years in a row.

In the fall of 1999, LeBron and his teammates from the Shooting Stars entered St. Vincent-St. Mary High School in Akron. The main reason the boys chose to attend this private school was that the basketball team was coached by Keith Dambrot, the former men's basketball coach at Central Michigan University. They believed Coach Dambrot was the top high school basketball coach in the city and they were anxious to play for him.

Compared to Magic Johnson

Dambrot was familiar with the success of the Shooting Stars and knew he was getting four talented basketball players. He was most impressed with LeBron. At the age of 15, LeBron had already grown to 6 feet 4 inches tall and 170 pounds. Dambrot was as impressed with LeBron's intelligence as he was with his skills and physical potential. He compared LeBron to Magic Johnson, the former Los Angeles Lakers superstar. He told Morgan:

> **"LeBron reminded me of an athletic Magic Johnson. He could rebound, pass, and defend. Physically, I had no idea he would develop like he did, but I knew mentally he had it. My feeling was that if he wanted to be the best ever, he had the talent to be, as long as he worked hard."**

In LeBron's first year playing for the St. Vincent-St. Mary Fighting Irish, the team cruised to a perfect 27–0 record. The team entered the Division III playoffs and soon advanced to the state championship game, which was played at Ohio State University in Columbus. LeBron was a major factor in the team's success, scoring 25 points in the title game. Dru Joyce III also had a big game, coming off the bench to score 21 points. The Fighting Irish easily defeated Jamestown Greenview High School to win the state championship.

In LeBron's sophomore year, he again led the team to a Division III state title, averaging 28 points, 7 rebounds, 6 assists, and 4 steals a game as the Fighting Irish finished with a 27–1 record. At the end of the season, the Ohio High School Basketball Coaches Association named him Mr. Basketball, the top award for high school players in the state. He also became the first sophomore to earn a place on *USA Today*'s All-USA First Team.

LeBron also excelled in football as a wide receiver for the St. Vincent-St. Mary squad. He was named to the All-State First Team, another rare honor for a sophomore. LeBron eventually decided to give up football, because he was concerned that he might get injured, and concentrate on his basketball career.

At the end of LeBron's sophomore year, he received some bad news from Coach Dambrot. The coach had agreed to join the staff at the University of Akron. LeBron and his teammates were very disappointed by Dambrot's departure. LeBron briefly considered transferring to another high school, but dropped those plans when he learned that the new St. Vincent-St. Mary coach would be someone very familiar: Dru Joyce II, his old coach from the Shooting Stars.

A picture of LeBron wearing the uniform of the St. Vincent-St. Mary High School Fighting Irish. He decided to attend the school because of the reputation of its basketball coach, Keith Dambrot. LeBron soon emerged as the best scholastic player in Ohio, leading the Fighting Irish to Division III state championships in his freshman and sophomore seasons.

LeBron rises above the rim during a high-school game. In 2001 he became the first sophomore to be named to the *USA Today* All-USA First Team basketball squad, averaging 27.8 points and 7.5 rebounds per game. He repeated this honor in his junior year, when he averaged 29.7 points and 8.4 rebounds per game.

The Next Superstar

When LeBron was a junior, the St. Vincent-St. Mary basketball games were drawing such large crowds that the school's home games had to be moved to the arena at the University of Akron. Also, that year St. Vincent-St. Mary was moved into Division II, where the Fighting Irish would have to compete against larger schools. This meant tougher opponents, but LeBron and his teammates again completed the season with an excellent record.

For the third time, St. Vincent-St. Mary made it to the state championship game. This time the Fighting Irish faced Roger Bacon High School from Cincinnati. More than 18,000 fans jammed into Ohio State University's Value City Arena to watch the two basketball powerhouses square off.

The game was close throughout. With less than 30 seconds left, Roger Bacon led 65 to 63. LeBron took the ball and drove the length of the court. Everyone in the arena expected LeBron to drive to the basket, but at the last moment he passed to an open teammate, Chad Mraz, who shot the ball from three-point range—and missed. The game ended in an upset victory for Roger Bacon. Asked by reporters why he had passed the ball instead of taking the shot, LeBron explained,

> **❝I just didn't want to force anything. Chad was open and I got him the ball. He could've put us up by one, but the whole year I've been looking for my teammates, so nothing was going to change.❞**

Despite the heartbreaking loss, LeBron was still regarded as one of the top high school athletes in the country. On February 18, 2002, *Sports Illustrated* featured LeBron on its cover, proclaiming him "The Chosen One." Making the cover of *Sports Illustrated* is a rare honor for even the best professional and college athletes. It is virtually unheard of for a high school athlete to be featured on the cover of the national magazine. Clearly, as LeBron prepared to enter his senior year in high school, many people felt the young athlete had a bright future ahead.

As a senior, LeBron was selected as Ohio Mr. Basketball—an award given to the best player in the state—for the third time. Although concerns about his eligibility caused him to miss several games, he was back in uniform in time to lead his team to a Division II state title.

3

Path to the NBA

A t 17 years old, LeBron James had emerged as the top high school basketball player in the nation. He could have had his pick of any top college basketball program in the country. However, LeBron was aware that his skills had already developed past the level of most college players, and that he was ready for the pros.

And so, as LeBron prepared for his last season with the Fighting Irish, he knew that in just a few short months he would be drafted by an NBA team and awarded with a contract that would make him a very wealthy young man.

By the time LeBron started his senior year at St. Vincent-St. Mary, he had reconnected with his mother and was again living in her home. Gloria James was her son's biggest fan. When Gloria attended his games, she wore a **jersey** that read, "LeBron's Mom." Eddie Jackson was also a familiar presence in LeBron's life, representing a father figure for the boy who had never known his real father.

For his 18th birthday, Gloria gave her son a special gift: an $80,000 luxury vehicle called a Hummer H2. However, the gift immediately raised suspicions among officials with the Ohio High School Athletic Association (OHSAA), the governing body for all high school sports in Ohio. While there is nothing wrong with a mother buying a gift for her son, Gloria was unemployed and could not afford the car. OHSAA officials wondered whether the car had really been purchased by a sports **agent** who wanted to represent LeBron when he entered into negotiations with an NBA team. The agent, who would earn a percentage of the player's contract, would stand to make millions of dollars if chosen by LeBron to represent him in the negotiations.

Severe Punishment

If it turned out a sports agent did buy the car for LeBron, the punishment could be quite severe. Under the OHSAA's rules, only **amateur** players can compete in Ohio high school games. This means that any player who accepts money or a gift worth more than $100 is ineligible. If he had accepted the Hummer from an agent, LeBron would be prohibited from playing any games in his senior year.

The OHSAA declared it would launch an investigation to find out who bought the car for LeBron. OHSAA Commissioner Clair Muscaro told reporters:

> **When our member schools see something like that, it throws up a red flag. It's different than a parent buying their son or daughter a small vehicle. If there is any chance that [the Hummer] was provided by an agent, [LeBron] would immediately lose his eligibility, and as far as we're concerned, that would be when he accepted the car.**

The investigation ultimately cleared LeBron and his mother of wrongdoing. It was determined that Gloria James had bought the car

Gloria James, wearing her special jersey, cheers her son during a 2003 game. During LeBron's senior season, the Ohio High School Athletic Association investigated whether a sports agent had given Gloria money to buy a luxury car for her son. The investigation eventually cleared Gloria and LeBron of any wrongdoing.

from a dealer in California who specializes in selling expensive automobiles to celebrities, professional athletes, and other wealthy people. Gloria had secured a bank loan to buy the car with the promise that after LeBron signed his NBA contract, he would pay off the loan. Under the OHSAA's rules, LeBron had not violated his amateur status by accepting the car from his mother.

But a gift that was much less expensive than the Hummer caused LeBron far more trouble. During the season, LeBron and some friends drove to Cleveland to watch a basketball game. While in the city, they dropped into a clothing store managed by a friend of Eddie Jackson's. After browsing in the store, LeBron stopped to say hello to the manager. As he was leaving, the manager gave LeBron replica jerseys that had been worn by former basketball star Wes Unseld and former football star Gale Sayers. The value of the two jerseys amounted to $845.

Two-Game Suspension

News of this gift eventually found its way to the OHSAA, which launched a new investigation. This time, there was no question that LeBron had been given an outright gift by somebody other than a family member. Muscaro declared that LeBron was now ineligible to play high school basketball in Ohio. He would have to sit out the remainder of the Fighting Irish season. LeBron was crushed. He felt as though he had let down his teammates. He said:

> **"I'm sorry. There's nothing I'm more sorry about, you know, than disrespecting my teammates. I love them to death. . . . I'm so proud of them, you know, to be able to stick it out for me."**

Gloria James hired an attorney to try to win back her son's eligibility. The attorney asked a local court in Akron to intervene. While waiting for the court to act, LeBron was forced to miss his first basketball game in more than three years. With LeBron sitting on the bench the Irish won the game against Canton McKinley High School, mostly through the efforts of Dru Joyce III, who had an outstanding game.

The following day the court ruled on LeBron's appeal. It found that his acceptance of the jerseys did violate OHSAA's rules, but reduced the penalty to a two-game suspension. After sitting out just

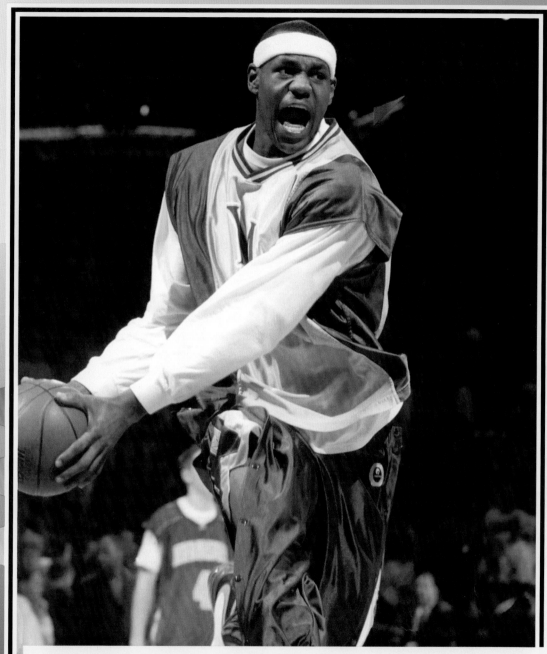

After LeBron accepted jerseys from a store owner in exchange for appearing in pictures that would be hung on the store's wall, the OHSAA declared him ineligible for the rest of his senior season. Instead of just turning pro, as he intended to eventually do anyway, LeBron fought the ruling so he would not let his teammates down.

LeBron James and Allyson Felix show off their trophies after being named the first Gatorade High School Athletes of the Year at an awards ceremony in July 2003. LeBron was honored for his accomplishments on the basketball court, while Allyson received the award for setting a track-and-field record in the 200 meter sprint.

one more game, LeBron was able to return to the basketball court for the Fighting Irish.

LeBron would lead St. Vincent-St. Mary to another state title. Once again, he was named Ohio Mr. Basketball and received a number of state and national honors, including selection as the *USA Today* High School Player of the Year and a McDonald's High School All-American. A few months after the end of the basketball season, LeBron accepted his diploma as a graduate of St. Vincent-St. Mary High School. He completed his senior year with a B average—quite an accomplishment for someone who, just a few years before, had been a poor student who often skipped school.

With his diploma in hand, it was time for LeBron to move on to a new chapter in his life.

Quick Bursts

As LeBron prepared to graduate from St. Vincent-St. Mary, the NBA's Cleveland Cavaliers were finishing another dismal season. Their poor finish, with a record of 17 wins and 65 losses, did provide the Cavs with one small measure of hope: the team would be guaranteed a place in the NBA draft **lottery**, a system that enables the league's worst teams the chance to draft the best talent coming out of college basketball, the European basketball leagues, or even top-notch high school programs.

The 14 teams eligible for the lottery are the teams that do not qualify for the NBA playoffs. Of those 14, the teams with the worst records are given the most opportunities in a lottery to win the best picks. When the 2003 lottery was conducted, the Cavaliers emerged with the top pick in the draft.

From the moment the team won the lottery, there was speculation that the Cavaliers would use the pick to select the amazing schoolboy athlete from nearby Akron. By now LeBron possessed the physical size and skills to compete in the NBA, having grown to 6 feet 8 inches tall and 250 pounds. But before officially committing to LeBron, Cavaliers officials wanted to see him up close for themselves. Shortly before the draft, they put LeBron through an hour-long workout at Gund Arena in Cleveland. They had him shoot from various places on the court, drive to the basket, rebound, and make passes. Supervising the workout was Austin Carr, a former Cavaliers star who now held an executive position with the team. After watching LeBron, Carr declared him ready for the NBA. He told reporters:

> **"He has the mobility, strength, quickness, and good short dribbles, which I didn't think he had from watching him play high school ball, because no one really challenged him. A guy his size who can have those quick short bursts, you can go where you want to go with the ball."**

On June 26, 2003, the NBA draft was held in New York's Madison Square Garden. It came as no shock when the Cavaliers made LeBron the top pick.

Marked Man

LeBron was not the first high school graduate to go right into the NBA. In years past, such stars as Moses Malone and Darryl Dawkins had passed up college to become professional basketball players right after high school. More recently, players such as Kobe Bryant, Kevin Garnett, Tracy McGrady, and Jermaine O'Neal have gone right into the NBA from high school.

LeBron was not even the first high school student to be selected as the first pick in the NBA draft. In 2001, the Washington Wizards had chosen Kwame Brown from Glynn Academy in Georgia with the top pick.

On the day of the draft, LeBron and his mother were invited to attend the event in New York. When NBA Commissioner David Stern announced his name as the first pick, LeBron strode up to the podium to shake hands with the commissioner and pose for photographs while wearing a white suit and a Cavaliers hat. Later, as he spoke with reporters, LeBron said he was well aware of the Cavaliers' high expectations for him. He said:

> **"I'm one of the highest-publicized players in the country right now and I haven't played one game of basketball in the NBA. I know I'm a marked man, but I just have to go out there and play hard and play strong every night with the help of my teammates."**

The Nike Contract

LeBron may have been a marked man, but he was also about to be a wealthy man. The Cavaliers rewarded their top pick with a three-year,

Holding his Cavaliers jersey, LeBron poses for photos after the 2003 NBA draft. When asked by reporters about being compared to such greats as Michael Jordan or Magic Johnson, LeBron said, "The hype is always going to be there for me because of the accomplishments I have made, but I'm setting goals for myself, not for anyone else."

$13 million contract. LeBron was in for an even bigger payday when Nike, a manufacturer of athletic shoes and equipment, signed him to a $90 million contract to **endorse** the company's basketball shoes.

LeBron's first TV commercial for Nike aired in early 2004. The commercial depicted a church service staged in a gym. The preacher, played by comedian Bernie Mac, announced the arrival of the "Chosen One."

"Can I get a lay-up?" shouted Mac, as the preacher.

"Lay up," responded the congregation.

Soon after turning pro, LeBron signed a $90 million deal to endorse Nike products. This shot from a television commercial is one of many advertisements he has done for the company. LeBron has also signed lucrative endorsement contracts with such companies as the soft drink brand Sprite, the sports drink Powerade, and the trading card firm Upper Deck.

LeBron then made his entry, funneling no-look passes to members of the audience who immediately broke for the basket. Meanwhile, two NBA legends—Jerry West and Julius Erving—sat quietly on stage, playing the roles of "church elders."

Clear Message

The commercial would prove to be controversial. In Dallas, Texas, a group of African-American **ministers** complained that the TV spot made fun of black church services, and they called for African Americans to **boycott** Nike shoes. One Dallas minister, Dr. Jerry Christian Sr., said, "It's very offensive, and the black church will not be used and exploited in this manner for money." The ministers garnered some national press with their complaints, but the boycott soon fizzled.

On the other hand, some people praised the commercial because it portrayed LeBron in a positive light. They pointed out that other African-American athletes, such as NBA star Allen Iverson, signed lucrative contracts with shoe companies, then marketed the sneakers by portraying tough, streetwise thugs in the commercials. Said National Public Radio commentator Seth Stevenson:

> **"Nike's gone clean-cut with LeBron. They've got him smiling, which is decidedly ungangsta, and perhaps most interesting, this whole spot is about LeBron's devotion to team, not about the jaw-dropping play-ground moves that often get used to sell sneakers. . . . It's a distinctive, almost humble image for LeBron."**

There was one other clear message contained in the commercial. Since the retirement of Michael Jordan following the 1998 season, the NBA had lacked that one special player who could rise above all the rest. Audiences accepted LeBron's Nike commercial as a statement that the NBA's next big superstar—"King James," the Chosen One—had arrived on the scene.

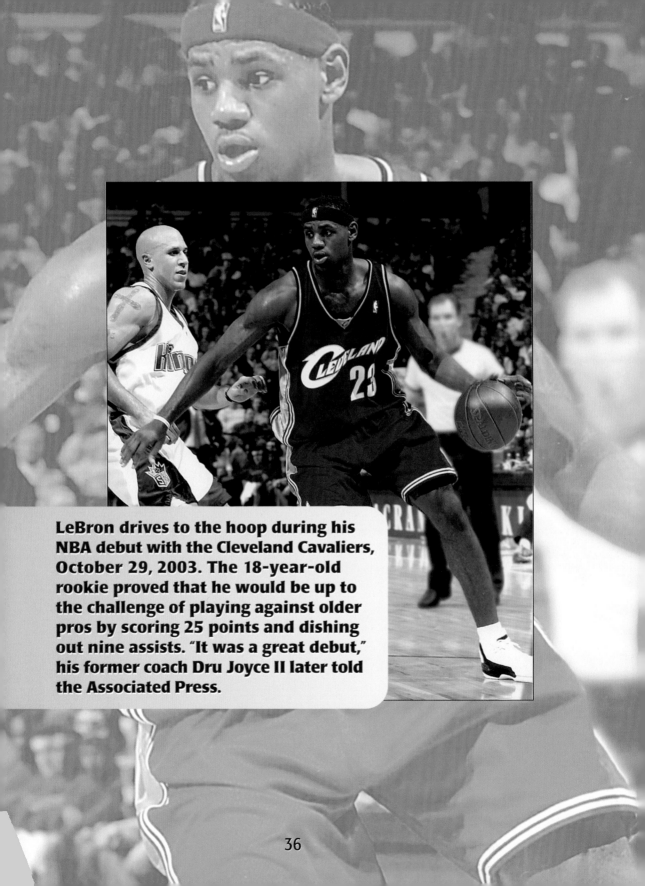

LeBron drives to the hoop during his NBA debut with the Cleveland Cavaliers, October 29, 2003. The 18-year-old rookie proved that he would be up to the challenge of playing against older pros by scoring 25 points and dishing out nine assists. "It was a great debut," his former coach Dru Joyce II later told the Associated Press.

4

International Star

The night that basketball fans had long anticipated arrived on October 29, 2003, when LeBron James made his NBA debut against the Sacramento Kings, one of the league's elite teams. Although the Cavaliers lost the game, players, coaches, and sportswriters all had high praise for the NBA's newest star. Sportswriter Tom Withers wrote:

"For one game, the Cleveland Cavaliers' 18-year-old rookie sensation soared above his mountainous hype with a breathtaking NBA debut Wednesday night at Sacramento. Facing one of the league's best teams, 17,000 screaming fans and enormous expectations,

'King James' proclaimed his arrival with 25 points, nine assists, six rebounds and four steals with a blend of flash and fundamentals.''

The game was nationally televised on ESPN, and an estimated 2.5 million TV viewers watched LeBron almost single-handedly keep the game competitive. As the first quarter drew to a close, the Kings had already built up a 12-point lead and were threatening to blow the game open. With the Kings in control of the ball, guard Mike Bibby made a pass to a teammate that was stolen by LeBron. He immediately passed the ball to Cavs forward Carlos Boozer, who went in for a dunk. Moments later, LeBron stole the ball again and this time jammed the ball home himself. Then he stole the ball a third time and passed to teammate Ricky Davis, who executed a thundering slam dunk.

One of the spectators in attendance was LeBron's old high school coach Dru Joyce II. After the game, Joyce said it did not surprise him that LeBron had refused to hog the ball and had passed so well to teammates. He said,

"Bron just wants to make his team better. He's not caught up in the stats. He cares more about winning than anything else. I know he's happy he played well, but I'm sure he would have liked to win."

As it turned out, LeBron's stellar performance against the Kings also made history. The 25 points LeBron scored that night were the most points ever scored by an NBA rookie who had entered the league right out of high school. The previous record had been 10 points, shared by Jonathan Bender of Indiana (1999) and Amare Stoudemire of Phoenix (2002).

Wealth and Acclaim

Signing with the Cleveland Cavaliers meant that LeBron would not have to leave his hometown of Akron, which is just a few miles south of Cleveland. After signing his contract, LeBron bought a comfortable home in an upscale Akron neighborhood. The house is far different from the modest homes he knew growing up in Elizabeth Park. The spacious house includes eight bathrooms, three fireplaces, and an in-ground swimming pool. Moving into the home with LeBron was his

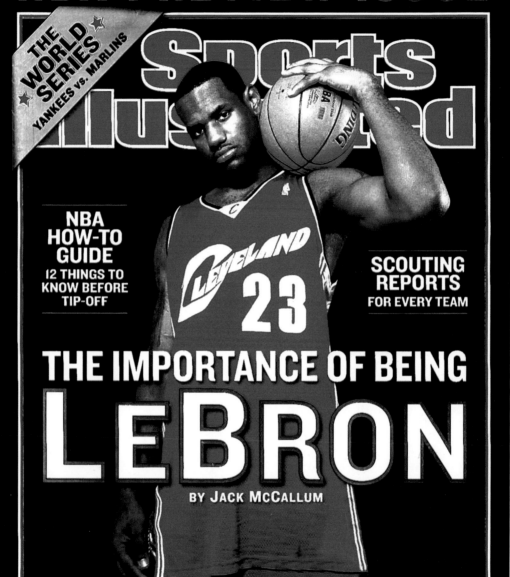

NBA PREVIEW ISSUE

THE WORLD SERIES YANKEES vs. MARLINS

Sports Illustrated

NBA HOW-TO GUIDE 12 THINGS TO KNOW BEFORE TIP-OFF

SCOUTING REPORTS FOR EVERY TEAM

CLEVELAND 23

THE IMPORTANCE OF BEING LeBRON

BY JACK McCALLUM

There was a great deal of excitement about LeBron's first season in the NBA. Many people looked to LeBron—dubbed "King James"—as a player who would restore the league's tarnished reputation after off-court misbehavior by such high-profile NBA stars as Allen Iverson and Kobe Bryant. LeBron was pictured on the cover of *Sports Illustrated's* 2003 preseason issue.

girlfriend from St. Vincent-St. Mary High School, Savannah Brinson. A baby boy soon arrived. The couple named him LeBron James Jr.

LeBron could easily afford the new home. The contracts he signed with the Cavaliers and Nike shoes made him a very wealthy man. Soon, his fortunes would be enhanced as other endorsement deals fell into place. LeBron eventually signed deals to endorse Bubblicious chewing gum, the soft drink Sprite, sports beverage Powerade, and the trading card company Upper Deck. His salary and endorsement deals were valued at about $125 million, giving him an annual salary of more than $20 million. Soon after signing his deals, *Forbes* magazine reported that LeBron was the 49th-highest paid celebrity in the United States. (He placed just behind Mary-Kate and Ashley Olsen but ahead of Renee Zellweger.)

The wealth, acclaim, and media attention hit LeBron like a whirlwind. As a senior at St. Vincent-St. Mary he had been exposed to a measure of national attention, but once his NBA rookie season started LeBron found himself the center of constant requests for interviews by reporters, autographs by fans, and other demands that accompany celebrities. The Cavaliers found themselves playing to sold-out arenas, not only in Cleveland but in other cities as well, as fans flocked to their games to get a glimpse of King James.

Throughout the year, LeBron did his best to keep his head on straight. During an interview with InsideHoops.com LeBron was asked how he handles all the attention. He responded:

> **"It's fun. I thank God for the God-given talent He gave me. I worked hard to get to the point where I'm at, and I'm happy to see the fans come out and watch us play. They come to see me, but they also got to see my teammates when we run up and down the court, and that's what I'm really thankful for."**

Not Quite an All-Star

LeBron went on to have a successful rookie season, averaging just under 21 points a game and earning Rookie of the Year honors. There were a few disappointments during the season, though. LeBron sprained his ankle in late January, which caused him to miss three games. Also, he was left off the Eastern Conference squad for the 2004 NBA All-Star Game in Los Angeles. By the All-Star break in February LeBron had

LeBron poses next to a race car decorated with his image and
the Powerade logo. The numerous endorsement deals that the
young athlete signed enabled LeBron to purchase a new home.
In late 2003 *Forbes* magazine reported that he was among the
highest-paid celebrities in the United States, earning more
than $20 million a year.

chalked up some impressive statistics, but other Eastern Conference players were having equally good years and, because of their experience, were given places on the squad.

LeBron did attend the All-Star Game and played in the annual Rookie-Sophomore Challenge, a tune-up to the main contest in which

Houston center Yao Ming and LeBron battle for the ball during the NBA All Star Rookie-Sophomore Challenge game, February 2004. LeBron dominated the game, scoring 35 points. At the end of his first season, LeBron became the youngest player in NBA history to be chosen Rookie of the Year, and finished ninth in voting for the league's Most Valuable Player.

many of the league's newest and brightest players get a chance to compete. Feeling he had something to prove because he had been left off the All-Star roster, LeBron played an intense game, scoring 35 points, grabbing five rebounds, and making six assists. He finished the game with some truly awesome slam dunks.

The main disappointment that season was Cleveland's failure to make the playoffs. There is no question that LeBron's arrival had improved the Cavaliers. The team that had won just 17 games the year before without LeBron won 35 games with him on the roster. It was a tremendous improvement, but the team still lost 47 games and finished in fifth place in the NBA's Central Division. Clearly, the Cavaliers still had plenty of room for improvement.

Olympic Team

Following the season, LeBron had little time to rest. He was selected to play on the U.S. team in the 2004 Olympic Games, which were staged in Athens, Greece. Although it is regarded as an honor to represent one's country in the Olympics, LeBron found himself with mixed emotions. The team included some of the best players in the NBA, and was coached by veteran Larry Brown, who did not believe in giving rookies extended court time. As a result, young stars like LeBron, Carmelo Anthony of the Denver Nuggets, and Dwayne Wade of the Miami Heat were mainly **benchwarmers** throughout the Olympics.

This was the first time since he had played for the Shooting Stars back in Akron that LeBron was not a starter. Later, he told the *New York Times*:

> **"I don't like that cliché, 'You lead by following.' I've always been a leader, I've never been a follower, so I've kind of just done my job and did the best every time I go out and just try to be a leader."**

The U.S. team did not play particularly well in Greece. Although the squad won the bronze medal by taking third place, that was a disappointment. The U.S. team had won the gold medal every year since 1992, when professionals were first allowed to play in the Olympics.

Trip to China

LeBron had a much better experience in 2006 when he was selected as one of three cocaptains (along with Anthony and Wade) for the U.S.

LeBron and a teammate on the U.S. Men's Basketball Team pose for a photo before the 2004 Summer Olympics. LeBron did not see much playing time during the Olympic Games, which were held in Athens, Greece. The star-studded American team was expected to win the competition, but finished a disappointing third overall.

Men's Basketball National Team for 2006 through 2008. When the team competed at the 2006 World Championships in Japan, it again won the bronze medal. However, the three young superstars dazzled the international audience that watched the series.

On the way to Japan, the team stopped first in Guangzhou, China, for an exhibition game. LeBron put on an impressive show for the Chinese—who know something about basketball because some top Chinese players, such as center Yao Ming of the Houston Rockets, have made it into the NBA. Still, Chinese fans were impressed by the spectacular play of the three young superstars from the United States. In the Guangzhou game—which the U.S. won by a score of 119 to 73—LeBron scored 22 points, many with slam dunks off the fast break. Following the game, LeBron told the Associated Press:

❝We are always going to be ready to play. The guys are bringing a lot of energy off the bench. We are producing on the court and taking care of business. We just had our stuff.❞

During the team's visit to China, LeBron took a brief side trip to a schoolyard in Guangzhou where he signed autographs. He even took lessons in Chinese before making the trip to China so he could say a few words to basketball fans there. "I had my note cards, my cheat sheets," he confided to a reporter during the trip.

With that type of enthusiasm for the sport, fans of Olympic basketball are expecting LeBron to help the American team win back the gold at the 2008 Olympics in Beijing, China.

A Chinese basketball fan stands with LeBron during a promotional event in Guangzhou, China, during August 2006. LeBron learned how to speak a few phrases in Mandarin Chinese for the trip, and he played well in an exhibition against the Chinese national team, scoring a game-high 22 points in the 119–73 victory.

"King James" slams a ball through the hoop in this multi-exposure photo. The young star revitalized the Cleveland franchise, which had been among the worst in the NBA before his arrival. The Cavaliers reached the playoffs in 2005–06 and again in 2006–07, with LeBron among the league's leading scorers both seasons.

5

Role Model for the Future

Following the Olympics, LeBron returned to Cleveland for the 2004–05 season and got down to work helping the Cavaliers improve. With LeBron averaging more than 27 points a game, the Cavaliers posted their first winning record since the 1997–98 season. Still, the team's record of 42 wins and 40 losses was not good enough to make the playoffs.

As for LeBron, he did make the All-Star team in 2005. He also made league history again when he scored 56 points in a game against the Toronto Raptors. LeBron was just 20 years old at the time, and he became the youngest player in NBA history to score 50 or more points in a game. The achievement was bittersweet, though, because the Raptors won the game. Afterward, LeBron told reporters:

> **"I don't care about individual stats, especially when you lose. I was disappointed to have as good a game as I had and still come out with a loss. It's a good achievement, but I'd rather set it with a win."**

As the 2005–2006 season got underway, fans in Cleveland as well as sportswriters, sportscasters, and other basketball experts expected the Cavaliers to finally make their move into the company of the NBA's elite teams. With LeBron now comfortable as one of the league's top talents, the Cavaliers made some moves in the off-season to surround him with better supporting players.

The Cavaliers did fulfill their promise and made the playoffs. They were led by LeBron, whose scoring average of 31.4 points per game was third-best in the league that year, behind scoring champion Kobe Bryant of the Los Angeles Lakers and Allen Iverson of the Philadelphia 76ers. His achievement qualified him for consideration as the league's Most Valuable Player and, in fact, he garnered quite a few votes for the honor, finishing second behind Steve Nash of the Phoenix Suns.

New Contract

In the summer of 2006, LeBron signed a contract extension with the Cleveland Cavaliers. The contract was very lucrative. It guaranteed him $60 million for three years, to commence after the completion of his rookie contract in the summer of 2007. LeBron said he signed the new contract to show his commitment to his fans in Cleveland and his nearby hometown of Akron. He told the *New York Times*:

> **"I am very excited and happy to be re-signing with the Cavaliers. Staying in Cleveland near my hometown of Akron provides me with the unique opportunity to continue to play in front of my family, friends and fans. I look forward to working toward bringing a championship to our great fans and the city of Cleveland."**

The new contract makes it possible for LeBron to become a **free agent** following the 2009–10 season. As a free agent, LeBron would be

LeBron blocks a shot by Luol Deng of the Chicago Bulls during a December 2005 game. During the 2005–06 season LeBron averaged more than 31 points per game, third-best in the NBA, and also averaged 7 rebounds and 6.6 assists per game. He finished second in MVP voting to Steve Nash of Phoenix.

allowed to sell his services to the highest bidder. Any team in the NBA would be eligible to make him an offer. With his talent and potential, that offer is expected to be of astronomical proportions. The Cavaliers had hoped to retain his rights longer. The team offered a five-year contract that guaranteed LeBron $80 million over the life of the deal. In accepting the shorter contract, LeBron took less money but he will now be able to enter the free agent market sooner.

Commitment to Cleveland and Akron

Although LeBron will one day have the freedom to sign with another NBA team, his commitment to Cleveland and Akron remains strong.

LeBron and other bikers line up for the start of the 2005 King for Kids Bike-a-Thon in Akron, Ohio. The event raises money for local charities, including the YMCA and the Urban League, and is one of several ways that LeBron has attempted to give something back to the community where he grew up.

Young people listen as LeBron speaks during a program on health and fitness. Unlike some NBA stars, who have cultivated a "gangsta" image or have gotten into trouble with the law, LeBron James has accepted the fact that he is a role model for young people and has always tried to present a positive image.

After he entered the league, LeBron and his mother Gloria established the James Family Foundation, which performs a number of charitable functions in northern Ohio. For example, in 2005 the foundation donated 1,000 backpacks filled with school supplies to needy students in Akron and Cleveland. The foundation also sponsors the annual "King for Kids Bike-a-Thon" in Akron. The event draws some 3,000 bicycle enthusiasts, who help raise money for the Akron Area

YMCA and the Akron Urban League. An enthusiastic bicycler himself, LeBron always participates, and he usually convinces other NBA stars to ride alongside him in the event. In a news release, Gloria James said:

> **"Starting the school year with a pencil, paper, and something to put it in was one thing I made sure LeBron had every school year. Now we want to help others by providing those same things."**

In addition, LeBron has lent his name to efforts to raise money for **prostate cancer** research. Prostate cancer has proven to be particularly widespread, afflicting one in six American men. The disease kills some 27,000 people a year. LeBron and other NBA stars have lent their names to specially produced wristbands; sponsors of the drive hope to sell 20,000 LeBron James wristbands at $3 each, which would raise $60,000 to help fund prostate cancer research.

LeBron also stepped forward to help the victims of Hurricane Katrina following the devastation caused by the storm in the summer of 2005. LeBron contributed some $200,000 to relief agencies, which used the money to buy food, water, clothing, building materials, and other supplies needed by the victims, who live along the coast of the Gulf of Mexico in Louisiana and Mississippi.

Raising His Profile

For now, LeBron remains committed to bringing Cleveland its first NBA championship. He did succeed in helping the Cavaliers return to the playoffs in the 2006–07 season, averaging more than 27 points, 6 rebounds, and 6 assists per game.

In the 2007 playoffs, the Cavs easily defeated their first two opponents, the Washington Wizards and the New Jersey Nets. This set up a payoff rematch with the rival Detroit Pistons in the Eastern Conference Finals. The first game of the series, held in Detroit, was a low-scoring affair between the two teams. With less than eight seconds remaining the Pistons held a two-point lead. LeBron drove toward the basket, but instead of taking a game-tying shot he passed to teammate Donyell Marshall, who was wide open behind the three-point line. However, Marshall missed the shot, and the Pistons escaped with a 79–76 win.

Afterward, many sportswriters criticized LeBron for not taking the final shot himself. LeBron defended his decision, saying:

> **"I go for the winning play. The winning play when two guys come at you and a teammate is open is to give it up. It's as simple as that."**

The next game was another disappointment for Cavaliers fans. Cleveland jumped out to a 50–38 lead in the first half, but Detroit clawed its way back. The lead changed hands several times during the fourth quarter, and the Pistons took a slim lead with just 10 seconds left. Once again, the Cavs got the ball to LeBron. This time he took the shot, but the ball clanged off the rim, and a Pistons' player eventually grabbed the rebound to seal another victory by a 79–76 score.

Coming from Behind

Down two games to none in the best-of-four series, LeBron and his teammates knew they had to win the next two games, which were played on their home court. LeBron delivered in Game Three, scoring 32 points and pulling down nine rebounds in an 88–82 Cavs victory. Another standout performance by LeBron in Game Four led to a 91–87 win, tying the series at two games apiece. LeBron scored 13 of his 25 points in the fourth quarter, and hit two crucial free throws with just second remaining to seal the victory.

Game five was another close contest for the first three quarters, but the Pistons pulled ahead by seven points with just over three minutes left to play. At that point LeBron took over. He scored 29 of his team's last 30 points as the Cavaliers emerged with a 109–107 double-overtime victory and the series lead. "We threw everything we had at him," commented Detroit star Chauncy Billups afterward. "We just couldn't stop him."

LeBron finished with 48 points, the most he had ever scored in the playoffs. Afterward, the exhausted star said:

> **"This is definitely a big win, one of the biggest wins in Cavaliers' franchise history. . . . But we have a goal, we can't dwell on this when we have another game on Saturday. We have got to do our best to try to win that ballgame and get where we wanted to be all year."**

LeBron drives to the basket past San Antonio Spurs defenders Bruce Bowen, left, and Tim Duncan, right, during Game 4 of the 2007 NBA Finals. Although LeBron made a good showing, the veteran Spurs were just too much for the Cavaliers, and San Antonio went on to claim another championship victory.

Reaching the Finals

The loss seemed to take the fight out of the Pistons. Game Six was not even close, with Cleveland winning 98–82. As the Cavaliers celebrated their victory, which put the team into the NBA Finals for the first time, LeBron commented:

"This is like a dream. This is probably the best feeling that I've ever had in my life."

A tough challenge awaited Cleveland in the finals. The San Antonio Spurs were one of the league's elite teams, and had won three championships in the previous eight years. The Spurs had relied on strong defense and scoring from stars Tim Duncan, Manu Ginobili, and Tony Parker to win 58 games in the regular season.

San Antonio's defense frustrated LeBron in the first game of the finals, holding him to just 14 points in an 85–76 Spurs victory. Although LeBron scored 25 points in the next game, the Spurs still won, 103–92. San Antonio ground out a 75–72 win in the third game, then nailed down their fourth championship with an 83–82 win.

Although the Cavaliers did not win the championship in 2007, LeBron James won many new admirers for his talent and desire to win. If he continues to work hard, anything is possible—even the NBA Title that has eluded the Cavaliers for so long.

1984   LeBron James is born December 30 in Akron, Ohio.

1987   LeBron's grandmother Freda dies on Christmas Day, forcing LeBron and his mother Gloria to find a new home.

1993   Joins the South Rangers, an Akron youth football league team, and scores 18 touchdowns in six games.

1994   LeBron misses 87 days of school in the fourth grade, then moves in with family friends Frank and Pam Walker, where he becomes a good student and dedicated athlete.

1995   Joins the Northeast Ohio Shooting Stars and leads the team to the first of three Amateur Athletic Union national competitions.

1999   Enters St. Vincent-St. Mary High School in Akron.

2000   Leads St. Vincent-St. Mary to a 27–0 record and a state high school basketball championship.

2001   Leads St. Vincent-St. Mary to a second state title.

2002   Appears on the cover of *Sports Illustrated*.

St. Vincent-St. Mary's bid for a third state title comes up one point short.

2003   After a brief suspension for accepting a gift from a store owner, leads St. Vincent-St. Mary to a third state title.

Selected first in the NBA draft by the Cleveland Cavaliers.

2004   Selected NBA Rookie of the Year.

Picked to play for the U.S. Men's Basketball Team at the Summer Olympics in Athens, Greece, but mostly sits on the bench as the squad wins the bronze medal.

First child, son LeBron James Jr., is born to LeBron and his girlfriend Savannah Brinson.

2005 Selected to play in the NBA All-Star Game.

2006 Leads the Cavaliers to their first playoff appearance in eight years.

Selected cocaptain of the U.S. Men's Basketball Team.

2007 Averages more than 27 points per game during the regular season, leading the Cavaliers back to the playoffs.

Cleveland reaches the NBA Finals, but falls to San Antonio in four games.

Second child, son Bryce Maximus James, is born to LeBron and Savannah Brinson.

Awards

2001 Mr. Basketball, Ohio High School Basketball Coaches Association.

USA Today All-USA First Team in Basketball.

Most Valuable Player, Adidas ABCD Camp Underclassman.

2002 Mr. Basketball, Ohio High School Basketball Coaches Association.

USA Today All-USA First Team in Men's Basketball.

USA Today High School Player of the Year.

Gatorade Circle of Champions National Boys Basketball Player of the Year.

2003 Naismith High School Player of the Year.

Most Valuable Player, McDonald's All-American Game.

McDonald's High School All-American.

McDonald's Morgan Wootten Award for National Player of the Year.

Most Valuable Player, EA Sports Roundball Classic.

Most Valuable Player, Jordan Capital Classic.

Most Valuable Player, Jeremy Nathaniel Memorial Classic.

USA Today High School Player of the Year.

Gatorade Circle of Champions National Boys Basketball Player of the Year.

USA Today All-USA First Team in Men's Basketball.

Mr. Basketball, Ohio High School Basketball Coaches Association.

Ohio Division II High School Player of the Year.

First player selected in the NBA draft.

2004 NBA Rookie of the Year.

Sporting News NBA Rookie of the Year.

NBA All-Rookie First Team.

Member, U.S. Men's Basketball National Team and winner of bronze medal at the Summer Olympics in Athens, Greece.

2005 East Squad, NBA All-Star Game.

All-NBA Second Team.

2006 East Squad, NBA All-Star Game.

NBA All-Star Game Most Valuable Player.

Sporting News NBA co-Most Valuable Player.

Co-captain, U.S. Men's Basketball National Team.

All-NBA First Team.

Career NBA Statistics

Season	G	ppg	rpg	apg	spg
2003–04	79	20.9	5.5	5.9	1.6
2004–05	80	27.2	7.4	7.2	2.2
2005–06	79	31.4	7.0	6.6	1.6
2006–07	78	27.3	6.7	6.0	1.6

Key:
G = games played
ppg = points per game
rpg = rebounds per game
apg = assists per game
spg = steals per game

Books

Fawaz, John. *NBA Superstars 2006*. New York: Scholastic Inc., 2005.

Finkel, Jon. *Future Stars of the NBA: Dwayne Wade, LeBron James, and Carmelo Anthony*. Los Angeles: Tokyopop Inc., 2005.

Jones, Ryan. *King James: Believe the Hype—The LeBron James Story*. New York: St. Martin's Griffin, 2003.

Mattern, Joanne. *LeBron James: Young Basketball Star*. Hockessin, Del.: Mitchell Lane Publishers, 2005.

Morgan Jr., David Lee. *LeBron James: The Rise of a Star*. Cleveland: Gray & Company Publishers, 2003.

Web Sites

www.ci.akron.oh.us

The city government of Akron, Ohio, maintains this Web site. Visitors can learn about the city and its history, take a virtual tour of the city, and read about other famous Akron natives, including model Angie Everhart, rock singer Chrissy Hynde, former football star Larry Csonka, Pulitzer Prize–winning poet Rita Dove, world-renowned yo-yo champion Linda Lorenz-Sengpiel, and Mina Miller, the wife of inventor Thomas Edison.

www.lebronjames.com

At LeBron James's official Web site, fans can receive updates on his statistics, review media coverage of the Cavs star, pose questions to James in an online forum, and read LeBron's online journal.

www.nba.com

The official Web site for the National Basketball Association, where fans can read news about the league and its teams, follow links to all teams in the league, and watch video highlights of selected games.

www.nba.com/cavaliers

Visitors to the Web site for the Cleveland Cavaliers can read news about the team, participate in on-line discussions about the Cavs, watch online videos of the team, and download wallpaper and screen savers featuring LeBron James and other players.

www.usabasketball.com

Official site of the U.S. Men's Basketball National Team, which will represent the United States at the 2008 Olympic Games as well as in other international competitions. Visitors to the site can find news about the team's activities, statistics, schedules, and brief biographies of LeBron James and other members of the squad.

agent—an individual who represents an athlete or other celebrity client in contract negotiations and typically receives a percentage—often 10, 15 or 20 percent—of the contract as payment for negotiating the deal. The more money the client receives, the more the agent receives.

amateur—in sports, an athlete who receives no pay to compete.

benchwarmer—a team member who does not play much, instead spending most of the game watching the action from the bench.

boycott—an organized attempt to convince people not to buy a product, usually made as a political statement or to encourage a corporation to alter a policy.

discipline—personal trait in which one follows rules and performs up to expectations without having to be prodded.

draft—in professional sports, a league program that enables the weakest teams to obtain the best amateur athletes.

endorse—backing given to a product by an athlete or other celebrity who is typically paid by the product's manufacturer to help sell the product. Typically, athletes fulfill their endorsement responsibilities by appearing in television commercials or other advertisements.

free agent—an athlete who has no contractual obligations to any team and is free to sell his or her services to the highest bidder.

jersey—athletic uniform shirt, typically featuring the number and name of the athlete who wears it.

lottery—a contest in which a single winner is selected from a large number of entries, typically drawn at random out of a hat or drum.

ministers—religious leaders who lead prayers and services in Protestant churches.

prostate cancer—a disease that affects a gland in the male urinary tract, and is often fatal if not treated in time.

tailback—in football, the player who takes the position behind the quarterback and, after the play begins, is most likely to carry the ball.

truant—a student who purposely stays away from school.

ABOUT THE AUTHOR

Hal Marcovitz lives in Chalfont, Pennsylvania, with his wife Gail and daughters Ashley and Michelle. He is the author of nearly 100 books for young readers, including *Lindsay Lohan* in the POP CULTURE: A VIEW FROM THE PAPARAZZI series.

Picture Credits

page

2: NBA/PRN Photos
6: NBA/AdMedia
9: NBA/AdMedia
10: Detroit Free Press/KRT
12: Phil Masturzo/MCT
15: KRT/MCT
17: Newswire Photo Service
18: Reuters Photo Archive
21: WENN Archive
22: KRT/MCT
24: Icon Sports Photos
27: TSN/Icon SMI
29: KRT/MCT
30: Newswire Photo Service

33: NBA/PRN Photos
34: New Millennium Images
36: NBA/PRN Photos
39: New Millennium Images
41: Newswire Photo Service
42: NBA/PRN Photos
44: UPI Newspictures
45: Cook Lau/ColorChinaPhoto
46: NBA/PRN Photos
49: Chicago Tribune/KRT
50: Aaron Beacon Journal/KRT
51: Newswire Photo Service
54: Aaron Beacon Journal/KRT

Front cover: Paul Fenton/KPA/Zuma Press
Back cover: NBA/PRN Photos